Herbal
& Yogic
Remedies

HAPPY MOTHER'S
GUIDE

Herbal
& Yogic
# Remedies

FOR COMMON AILMENTS

Also Health Myths and Facts

Dr. Hitendra Ahooja

wisdom
tree

ISBN 81-86685-08-1

Published by
Wisdom Tree
A 23 Mayapuri II
New Delhi 110 064
011-513 0720, 549 1437

Printed at
Print Perfect
New Delhi 110 064

INTRODUCTION

Man's quest for good health is as ancient as the beginning of life itself. Over the centuries man has used ways and means that would provide comfort and healthy life. But, with the advent of civilization came an extravagant lifestyle coupled with illnesses and diseases. With this began a new crusade —a crusade against diseases and to unravel the secrets of good health. Modern medicine offers cure for various illnesses but is silent on providing practical tips to tide over daily health problems. It is said that if you treat a cold it gets cured in a week and if you don't it would probably take seven days! All of us have heard of this maxim and experienced it first hand, but ask your Granny and she can probably provide concoctions and remedies to comfort you in a matter of hours. Armed with herbal remedies which have been passed and tested through generations, she has a ready cure for all common ailments.

This book not only offers a combination of herbal and yogic remedies, which have been an integral part of Indian system of medicine but also explains the various fallacies and myths that we live with.

Written by a qualified doctor, the book suggests treatments for common ailments through natural foods and substances which are readily available at home or are within easy reach. Usually, without any side effects, these remedies don't just curb the symptoms (as modern medicine does) but build the body's resistance against the disease, making you stronger and healthier from within.

So make yoga a way of life and with the help of natural remedies live a healthier and happier life.

CONTENTS

REMEDY FOR

ACNE

- Usually acne occurs when skin gets clogged with oil and bacteria. Orange peel has been found very effective in the local treatment of acne. Pounded well with water on a piece of stone, the peel should be applied to the affected areas.

- The juice of lemon if applied regularly, provides considerable relief.

- Garlic has been used successfully in the treatment of acne. Pimples disappear without scars when rubbed with raw garlic several times a day.

- Salicylic acid is a clarifying agent for the skin. Since cloves contain salicylic acid, a face pack for pimples should contain cloves as an essential ingredient.

1

MYTHS

Sweets and chocolates aggravate acne problems.

FACTS

A research by the Yale School of Medicine found that eating chocolate made no appreciable difference to the extent or the severity of acne.

ALLERGIES

- Five drops of castor oil added to half a cup of any fruit or vegetable juice, or plain water, and taken on an empty stomach early in the morning, is beneficial for allergies of intestinal tract, skin and nasal passages.

- Lime juice provides an effective remedy for any kind of allergy. Half a lime is squeezed in a glass of lukewarm water and sweetened with a teaspoon of honey for drinking early in the morning.

- One or two bananas a day are useful for those who are allergic to certain foods and who constantly suffer from skin rashes, digestive disorders or asthma.

- To reduce severe itching, apply ice on the affected part.

MYTHS

Allergies are caused by eating high protein foods.

FACTS

It is not the high protein foods like milk, cheese, etc. which cause allergy but how long you have kept it outside and not at proper low temperature that is actually responsible.

ANAEMIA

- The leaves of fenugreek (*methi*) help in blood formation as they contain iron.

- Lettuce is another effective remedy for this ailment as it contains a considerable amount of high grade iron. On absorption, it helps in the formation of haemoglobin and red blood cells.

- Spinach is a leafy vegetable which is rich in iron. On absorption, it helps in the formation of haemoglobin.

MYTHS

Anaemia occurs in thin, undernourished people.

FACTS

Anaemia occurs due to loss of iron and can affect fat people also whose intake of iron is not adequate.

ANAEMIA

Paschimottanasana

This *asana* is useful in curing anaemia.

1. Sit with legs stretched, toes turned inwards.
2. Cross both the arms along the sides of the trunk near the armpit.
3. Bend slightly backward and inhale
4. When exhaling, bend the body forward with arms stretched in front to reach out for your toes, with head   bent down.
5. Withdraw the arms back to the armpits when inhaling, and return to the original

4

ARTHRITIS

- Raw potato juice is beneficial in curing arthritis considerably. Cut a medium sized potato into thin slices and without peeling the skin, place the slices overnight in a large glass filled with cold water. This water should be drunk the next morning on an empty stomach.

- A teaspoon of black sesame seeds, soaked in a quarter cup of water and kept overnight, has proved effective in preventing frequent joint pains.

- Garlic with its anti-inflammatory properties, is another effective remedy for countering arthritis. Two cloves of garlic should be taken daily on an empty stomach.

5

MYTHS

Vitamins provide energy.

FACTS

Calories from fat, carbohydrates and proteins provide energy. Vitamins don't have calories, so supply no extra energy.

ARTHIRITS

Virabhadrasana

This *asana* is useful in curing arthritis.

1. Stand with feet apart.
2. Extend the arms on the sides parallel to the floor with the palms facing the floor.
3. Slowly lift the forefoot of the right leg, turn the leg sideways towards the right side with the right knee facing the right side and then place the foot on the floor.
4. Bend the right knee in such a way that the outer Knee and the heel of that leg are in the same line and form a perpendicular line to the floor.
5. Turn the head towards the right and look towards the right side. Remain in this posture for 30 seconds.
6. Repeat the same with the other leg.

6

ASTHMA

- Boil a teaspoonful of Bishop's weed seeds (*ajwain*) in a cup of water. Add a little salt to it and take this decoction at least once a day for quick relief.

- Among fruits, figs have proved very useful in controlling asthma.

- One or two teaspoons of honey prove helpful in asthma.

MYTHS

Fasting flushes out impurities and toxins.

FACTS

No evidence proves this. The body was designed to process food and removes naturally occurring toxins.

ASTHMA

Siddhasana :

This *asana* is useful in curing asthma.

1. Sit with legs stretched forward.
2. Bend the left leg, and place it near the perineum. The sole of the left foot is placed under the right thigh.
3. Bend the right leg, place the right foot over the left ankle, and the heel of the right foot at the root of the genitals.
4. Maintain the spine, neck and head in a straight, upright posture. Place both hands near the thigh joints, slightly bent at the elbows on either side with the middle fingers and thumbs of the two hands touching each other respectively.
5. Slowly bend the neck, downwards and allow the chin to touch the bottom of the throat.
6. Breathe normally, remain in this pose for 30 seconds.
7. Repeat this five times.

8

BACKACHE

- Oil is prepared with 5 to 6 cloves of garlic mixed in 2 to 3 tbsp of mustard/coconut oil and heated till the cloves become black. When rubbed on the back the mixture provides great relief to the back.

- The juice of one lemon mixed with common salt mixed in a glass of water should be taken twice daily to get relief from backache.

- Application of raw potato on the back is also a useful remedy.

MYTHS

Sugar causes diabetes

FACTS

Foods that produce high blood sugar level, may increase the risk of diabetes but sugar has only a moderate effect on blood sugar level.

BACKACHE

Dhanurasana

This *asana* is useful in curing backache.

1. Bend both legs at the knees and raise the head and chest.
2. Catch hold of the legs firmly at the ankles with respective hands.
3. Pull the ankles upward while inhaling, lifting the thighs off the floor. Only the abdomen and pelvis remain in contact with the floor. The spine looks like a stretched bow.
4. Try to keep the knees together and retain the pose for six seconds.
5. Release the hold on the ankles when exhaling and stretch the legs fully.

BODYACHE

a. Boil ten basil *(tulsi)* leaves in one cup of water till the quantity is reduced to half a cup. After cooling add salt to the liquid decoction. Take this mixture daily to stop bodyache

b. Alternatively, take half a gram of *dalchini* powder with one teaspoonful of honey at least twice a day for quick remedy.

11

COMMON COLD

- Mix a gram of *dalchini* powder with a teaspoonful of honey and drink it. This will help to curb a cold.

- Prepare a cup of tea to which you could add ginger, clove, bay leaf and black pepper. This should be consumed twice a day.

- Garlic soup (4 to 5 crushed cloves of garlic are boiled in 1 cup of water with a pinch of salt and honey added to it) is another remedy to reduce the severity of a cold, and should be taken once daily.

- To get rid of an irritating cold in no time, eat a pinch of blackpepper in the night before turning in.

MYTHS

Sweating rids the body of toxins.

FACTS

Sweating does eliminate some of the toxins, but sweat is about 99% water, rest is salt, fat molecules, Vitamin C and lactic acid.

COMMON COLD

Sirasana

This *asana* is useful in curing common cold, cough.

1. Kneel on the floor, and lean forward. Rest the elbows on the floor and interlock the fingers.
2. Keep the top of the head in between the clasped hands and elbows.
3. Exhale, and slowly lift the legs by first resting on the toes and then stretching upwards, toes pointing towards the sky.
4. Remain in the head stand posture for 20 seconds. Breathe normally
5. Repeat three times.

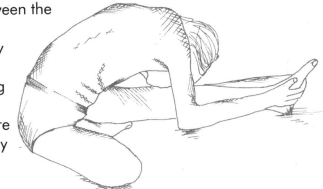

COMMON FEVER

- A decoction made of about 12 grams of basil leaves, boiled in half a litre of water, if administered twice daily with half a cup of milk, one teaspoon of sugar and a quarter teaspoon of powdered cardamom is an effective cure for lowering fever.

- Tea made from fenugreek seeds is very effective in reducing fever.

- Tea made from saffron is another effective home remedy for fever. This tea is prepared by dissolving half a teaspoon of saffron in water and having this tea every hour till the temperature falls.

MYTHS

Drinking water during meals hinders digestion.

FACTS

Its important to drink enough fluids but not necessarily at meals. The stomach needs fluid to digest food, but it draws that from the rest of the body temporarily. Also everything we eat contains water.

REMEDY FOR

COUGH

a. Add a gram of turmeric powder to a teaspoonful of honey for curing dry cough.

b. Chew a cardamom for a long time.

c. Almonds are also very useful for curing cough. When soaked overnight in water the brown skin can be removed easily and the almonds can be grinded into a fine paste before being eaten.

d. A mixture of one teaspoon ginger juice and one teaspoon honey taken three times a day gives instant relief from chest congestion.

e. *Sirasana (see page 13) is useful in curing cough.*

MYTHS

If you eat low fat foods, you will not get fat.

FACTS

A low fat cheese sandwich with salad covered in low fat mayonnaise followed by low fat ice cream can add to a lot of fat and calories.

DANDRUFF

- Use of fenugreek seeds is one of the most important remedies in the treatment of dandruff. Two tablespoons of these seeds are soaked overnight in water and ground into a fine paste with curd the next morning. This paste is applied all over the scalp and left for half an hour. The hair is then washed with soap-nut (*ritha*) or *shikakai* powder

- The use of a teaspoon of fresh lime juice for the last rinse, while washing the hair, is another useful remedy.

- Massage hot oil mixed with cedar vinegar in hot water all over the scalp. Leave it overnight and rinse off with an egg shampoo the next morning.

- Put a few drops of lime juice in coconut oil and massage your hair with it to get rid of dandruff.

MYTHS

Organically grown vegetables are more nutritious than vegetables grown with commercial facilities.

FACTS

If the soil is rich enough to support plants then it is immaterial whether the nutrients are organic or chemical in origin.

DEFECTIVE VISION

- Increase in intake of vitamin A is of utmost importance for improving vision. The best sources of this vitamin are spinach, turnip tops, milk cream, cheese, butter, tomatoes, lettuce, carrots, cabbage, soya beans, green peas, fresh milk, oranges and dates.

- *Triphala* is also considered beneficial in overcoming defective vision. Mix *triphala* in a litre of water and drink daily or use it for washing the eyes by pouring in an eye-cup and fluttering the eyelids in it.

MYTHS

Reading fine print or doing detailed work will weaken your eyes.

FACTS

It is not print but bad posture and poor light that are responsible for weak eyesight. Lack of Vitamin A is also responsible for poor eyesight.

DEFECTIVE VISION

Bhujangasana

This *asana* is useful in fighting flatulence, defective vision.

1. Lie on your abdomen, legs stretched and toes pointing outwards. Bring the hands just below shoulders.
2. With the aid of arms, slowly raise the upper portion of the body above the waist while inhaling.
3. Return to starting position when exhaling before retiring To rest.

DEPRESSION

- Apple is one of the most valuable remedies for overcoming mental depression.

- Cashewnut *(kaju)* is a valuable dryfruit for fighting general depression and nervousness.

- Use of cardamom *(elaichi)* has proved valuable in curing depression. Powdered seeds should be boiled in water and tea prepared in the usual way.

MYTHS

Drinking liquids while exercising or right after exercise is harmful.

FACTS

It is advisable to drink salt dissolved in water because during and after exercise there is loss of salt through excessive perspiration and the loss needs to be replaced.

DIABETES MELLITUS

- Among the several home remedies that have proved beneficial in controlling diabetes, perhaps the most important one is the use of bittergourd. For best results, the diabetic should take the juice of about four or five *karelas* every morning on an empty stomach.

- Indian gooseberry, with its high vitamin C content, is considered valuable in curing diabetes.

- Eating a grapefruit every day helps in reducing the blood sugar level.

MYTHS

Food Groups should never be combined in a meal.

FACTS

There is no evidence to support this contention. Our digestive system handles food combinations very effectively.

DIABETES MELLITUS

Janusirasana

This *asana* is useful in diabetes mellitus, diarrhoea.

1. In a sitting position, stretch out the left leg and bend the right leg in such a manner that the sole touches the left thigh, with the heel exerting pressure on the perineum.
2. Keep the trunk and head erect and breathe in.
3. With exhalation, bend the head forward and downward towards the knees and extend forward the forearms and fingers towards the extended left leg as much as is convenient.
4. When inhaling, return to the upright sitting position and straighten the folded leg.
5. Repeat the movements with the right leg stretched out.

REMEDY FOR

DIARRHOEA

- Buttermilk is one of the most effective treatments for curing diarrhoea. The acid in the buttermilk helps fight germs and bacteria.

- Carrot soup is another effective treatment of diarrhoea.

- Fenugreek leaves are also useful. One teaspoon of these seeds which have been boiled and fried in little butter should be taken with a cup of buttermilk twice daily.

- *Janusirasana (see page 21) is useful in curing diarrhoea.*

MYTHS

Wheat bread has more fibre than white bread.

FACTS

Only if it is "whole wheat" bread. Otherwise wheat and white bread are essentially the same. Both are made from white flour.

REMEDY FOR

DIZZINESS

- Thyme if taken daily, proves an excellent cure for dizziness.
- People suffering from frequent dizzy spells are advised to drink sage tea sweetened with honey.
- A drink made from cowslips boiled in water, with honey added to taste is another effective remedy.

MYTHS

Eating cheese is not good for teeth.

FACTS

Rather, all cheeses contain phosphate and a compound called casein, which binds with calcium to shore up tiny cracks in your teeth.

EARACHE

- Use of garlic has been found beneficial in the treatment of earache. Three cloves are warmed and crushed with a pinch of salt. This mixture is wrapped in a piece of woollen cloth and placed on the painful ear.

- Basil leaves are also considered beneficial for earache. The juice of these leaves is extracted by cooking in water and putting two to three drops in the ear.

- Heat mustard oil and put 2 to 3 drops in your ear. The earache will gradually disappear.

- Place a little *asafoetida* wrapped in a small piece of cloth in the ear. The ear ache will vanish.

MYTHS

Removing blackheads will cause scarring.

FACTS

This practice neither enlarges the pores nor leaves any scars.

24

FATIGUE

- A person suffering from fatigue should take lots of cereal seeds like those of corn wheat, rye, maize, barley and oat.

- Besides containing plenty of vitamins and minerals, dates are effective in removing fatigue. Five to seven dates are soaked overnight in half a cup of water and crushed in the morning in the same water after removing the seeds. This water with the essence of dates should be taken at least twice a week.

- Fatigue may cause bodyache and lethargy. Soak yourself in hot water or take a warm-water bath to rejuvenate yourself

25

MYTHS

Earwax build up is dangerous.

FACTS

Earwax is actually the body's own protection against dust and other irritants, as well as against possible sources of infection such as fungi and bacteria.

FLATULENCE

- Peppermint, cinnamon and ginger are found useful in the treatment of flatulence.

- Cloves, barley, carrots and onions are effective in reducing flatulence.

- Thyme, lavender, olive oil and eucalyptus are other known remedies for flatulence.

- Curd is an excellent antacid; just eat a few spoonfuls when acidity hits you.

- Make a paste of one teaspoon *asafoetida* and half a teaspoon water and apply on the navel to get rid of gas problems

- *Bhujangasana (see page 18) is useful in curing flatulence.*

26

MYTHS

If you eat late at night, the food turns straight into fat

FACTS

No, but it may cause indigestion or heartburn and keep you awake.

FOOD POISONING

- Early herbalists used garlic in cases of food poisoning.
- Castor oil is used to cure this.

MYTHS

A good toothpaste is most important for dental hygiene.

FACTS

Rather, it is the brush and the method of brushing which are more important.

GASTRITIS

- Coconut water is an excellent remedy for gastritis. It gives the stomach necessary rest and provides vitamins and minerals.

- Consuming rice gruel is another excellent remedy.

- Potato juice has been found to be valuable in curing the ailment. Half a cup of the juice taken two or three times daily is very effective.

MYTHS

It takes twenty minutes of exercise to start burning fat.

FACTS

The fact is that the body is always burning fat, even while sleeping. Fat is burned during any type of activity such as walking, running, dancing, talking etc. The key to losing weight is burning calories.

REMEDY FOR

HEADACHE

- Lemon is beneficial in the treatment of headache. Juice of three or four slices of lemon should be squeezed in a cup of tea and taken whenever headache occurs.

- Apples are valuable in all types of headaches. After removing the upper rind and the inner hard core of a ripe apple, it should be taken with a little salt every morning on an empty stomach.

- Cinnamon is useful in headaches caused by exposure to cold air.

- Half a teaspoon of ginger paste applied on the forehead helps in getting rid of a nagging headache.

MYTHS

Menopause and weight gain go together.

FACTS

The real culprit is slow metabolism due to age. As one ages, the body needs fewer calories to maintain weight.

HEADACHE

Halasana

This *asana* is useful in headaches, high blood pressure.

1.   Lie on you back, arms resting on respective sides.
2.   Raise both the legs slowly without bending the knees, when inhaling
3.   Raise the hips and lower the legs towards the head and then beyond it. Exhale slowly.
4.   Let the toes touch the ground.
5.   Arms should be returned to their original position.
6.   Return to starting position when Inhaling.

REMEDY FOR

HEAD LICE

- Cinnamon applied externally as a hair-wash helps to get rid of head lice.
- A non-herbal treatment to get rid of nits is to mix kerosene and water in equal parts and apply to the hair.
- Rosemary oil is also thought to be helpful in the treatment of head lice.

MYTHS

Running shoes with big spongy soles are better.

FACTS

Rather overly thick soles cause a loss of balance and may lead to ankle sprains and injuries.

HICCUPS

- Take a warm slice of lemon and sprinkle salt, sugar and black pepper to it. The lemon should be eaten till the hiccups stop.

- A very old cure for hiccups is a hot infusion of white mustard seeds.

- Another remedy involves placing the fingers in the ears and drinking a lot of cold water.

- Chewing a few radish leaves will help to stop an attack of hiccups.

MYTHS

If you stop working out to burn calories, then muscle gets converted to fat.

FACTS

When you stop working out you continue to eat the same way as earlier, but do not expend calories. As a result body fat increases which is why you put on weight on stopping exercise.

HIGH BLOOD PRESSURE

- Garlic is regarded as an effective means of lowering blood pressure. It may be taken in the form of raw cloves, two to three capsules a day.

- A tablespoon each of fresh *amla* juice and honey mixed together is very effective in high blood pressure.

- Watermelon is another valuable safeguard against high blood pressure. The seeds, dried and roasted, should be taken in liberal quantities.

- *Halasana (see page 30) is useful in curing high blood pressure.*

MYTHS

Potatoes with a green tint should be discarded.

FACTS

Not necessarily, granted, the green tint comes from a pigment called chlorophyll, peeling away the green layer to a depth of 1/8 inch will do away with unwanted substances.

INDIGESTION

- Ginger and peppermint are popular cures for indigestion. The juice of a raw potato taken as a drink can also cure indigestion.

- Olive oil and cardamom seeds can be used to treat indigestion. Parsley and burdock taken internally are also beneficial.

- Eating a ripe papaya with a pinch of cumin powder, pepper and salt cures constipation and indigestion.

- Dry grind and store 100gram cumin seeds, 100 gram aniseeds, 50 gram caraway seeds and 100 gram candy sugar. Take half a teaspoon of this mixture regularly after meals.

34

MYTHS

When you are just going to get an infection, foods which give you a quick energy high help.

FACTS

Rather, they drain you in the long term, for e.g. just a spoonful of sugar produces the responses of infection fighting white blood cells by half.

REMEDY FOR

INJURY

- For any cut, or wound, apply turmeric powder to the injured portion to stop the bleeding. It also works as an antiseptic. You can tie a bandage after applying *haldi.*

- Heat milk and cook one teaspoon turmeric powder in it. Mix sugar or honey and drink before retiring for the day and early morning. It helps to heal injuries faster.

MYTHS

Freezing destroys bacteria in food.

FACTS

Although growth stops and total bacterial count may decline during freezing, plenty of microbes will still survive.

REMEDY FOR

ITCHING

- Apply *neem* oil to the affected area. Or make a fresh paste of some *neem* leaves and apply externally. Boil *neem* leaves in hot water and take a bath in it. Also eat a teaspoon of *neem* juice along with sugar for quick relief.

- Another cure is to rub a weak carbolic acid lotion or a solution of bicarbonate of soda.

- To reduce severe itching, apply ice on the affected part.

MYTHS

People with kidney stones should avoid calcium rich foods.

FACTS

Rather, due to the effect of dietary calcium on oxalates in the intestine the opposite might be true.

REMEDY FOR

INSOMNIA

- Of the various food elements, thiamine is of special significance in the treatment of insomnia. Valuable sources of this vitamin are wholegrain cereals, pulses and nuts.

- Milk is very valuable in curing insomnia. A glass of milk, sweetened with honey, should be taken every night before going to bed.

- Curd is also useful in insomnia. The patient should take plenty of curd and massage it on the head. This induces sleep.

MYTHS

To build muscles a high protein diet is essential, so taking supplements is necessary.

FACTS

Excess protein in the body is converted to fat and puts excessive load on the kidneys that handle waste matter. A supplement should be taken to add to your diet on not getting a balanced meal because you are constantly on the go.

INSOMNIA

Sarvangasana

This *asana* is useful in fighting piles, insomnia, tonsilitis.

1. Lie with supine body at full length, arms on respective sides. Take a deep breath.
2. Fold the legs, slowly exhale and with a little jerk, raise the lower part of the body, pushing up from buttocks and holding the waist with hands.
3. Balance entire body weight upon the palms, the elbows, the neck and back of the head.
4. Fold the legs at the knee or raise the leg, whatever is convenient and easily manageable.
5. Maintain the position with slow, normal rhythmic breathing for not more than two minutes.
6. Slowly come back to the starting position with inhalation.

INTESTINAL WORMS

- Coconut is very effective in the treatment of intestinal worms. A tablespoon of freshly ground coconut should be taken at breakfast, followed by castor oil mixed in lukewarm water.

- Carrots are valuable in the elimination of thread worms among children as parasites find carrots offensive.

- The digestive enzyme pepsin in the milky juice of unripe papaya is a powerful agent for destroying roundworms.

MYTHS

Only a plastic cutting board is safe.

FACTS

Any cutting board is fine, so long as its scrubbed thoroughly with soap and water after exposing to meat, fish, poultry and their juices.

JAUNDICE

- Green leaves of radish is a valuable remedy for curing jaundice. The leaves should be pounded and their juice extracted before sieving through fine muslin cloth.

- Tomatoes are valuable in curing jaundice. A glass of fresh tomato juice, mixed with a pinch of salt and pepper, and taken early in the morning, is considered an effective remedy for jaundice.

MYTHS

House plants reduce pollution.

FACTS

They may have some effects, but don't rely on them to solve real problems like cigarette smoke or carbon monoxide.

KIDNEY STONES

- Apples are useful in getting relief in kidney stones.

- Grapes have an exceptional diuretic value on account of their high contents of water and potassium salt.

- Seeds of both sour and sweet pomegranates prove a useful medicine for kidney stones. A tablespoon of the seeds, ground into a fine paste, can be given along with a cup of *kulthi* soup to dissolve the gravel in kidneys.

MYTHS

Too much salt causes pre-menstrual bloating.

FACTS

The reason, salt, or, more specifically, the sodium in salt, doesn't appear to have an impact is that several days before menstruation begins, women excrete more salt in their urine than usual.

LOSS OF HAIR

- A vigorous rubbing of the scalp with fingers after washing the hair with cold water is one of the most effective among home remedies for prevention and treatment of loss of hair.

- *Amla* oil, prepared by boiling the dry pieces of *amla* in coconut oil, is a valuable hair tonic for enriching hair growth.

- Lettuce is useful in preventing hair loss. A mixture of lettuce and spinach juice can help the growth of hair.

MYTHS

Diabetics should avoid carbohydrates.

FACTS

If eating a certain level of carbohydrates allows a person to get his or her blood sugar level into the desired range, consuming even less will not control blood sugar any better.

LOW BLOOD PRESSURE

- The juice of raw beetroot is one of the most effective treatments for low blood pressure. A cup of this juice should be taken twice daily.

- Protein, Vitamin C, and all vitamins of the B group are beneficial in checking low blood pressure.

- Use of salt is also valuable in controlling low blood pressure. Till the blood pressure returns to normal, salty foods should be taken.

MYTHS

Athletes need much more protein than other people.

FACTS

Muscles are indeed made of protein, but consuming extra amounts of it in the form of lots of meat, protein powder drinks or amino acid supplements will not add to their bulk or strength. The only way to build muscle is to place extra stress on it through physical activity.

Padmasana

This *asana* is useful in curing low blood pressure.

1. Sit with legs stretched forward.
2. Fold one leg (whichever is convenient) and place the foot on the opposite thigh, heel pressing the pubic bone.
3. Similarly, bend the other leg in a way that the ankles cross each other. In this way, each foot is on the opposite thigh with the soles turned upwards—the two heel ends almost touching each other—knees pressed to the ground. Rest the palms on respective knees.
4. Keep the spine erect and neck straight.
5. Place left hand with its back touching the two heels and then place the right hand overlapping this. Keep eyes fixed on any object in front or keep eyes closed or gaze at the tip of your nose and concentrate.

MALARIA

- Grapefruit is one of the most effective home remedies for malaria. It should be taken daily.

- Cinnamon(*dalchini*) is an effective remedy for curing malaria. One teaspoon should be coarsely powdered and boiled in a glass of water with a pinch of pepper powder and honey.

- Lime and lemon are also effective in bringing down malarial fever. About three grams of lime should be dissolved in about 60 ml of water followed with the juice of a lemon added to it.

MYTHS

Sugar is the worst thing for diabetics.

FACTS

Sugar and sugary foods in normal servings have no greater effect on blood sugar levels than many starchy foods. Saturated fat is far worse for people with diabetes.

MIGRAINE

- Juice of ripe grapes if consumed at regular intervals proves an effective cure for migraine.

- Niacin has proved helpful in the treatment of migraine. Valuable sources of this vitamin are yeast, whole wheat, green leafy vegetables, tomatoes, nuts, sunflower seeds, liver and fish.

- Carrot juice, in combination with spinach juice, or beet and cucumber juices, has been found beneficial in the treatment of migraine.

MYTHS

The sniff test will ensure food safety at home.

FACTS

A keen nose can often detect outright spoilage, but it cannot detect small amounts of bacteria. A food that smells okay can still make you sick if inadequately cooked.

46

REMEDY FOR

NAUSEA

- Ginger and peppermint have long been held to be excellent cures for nausea.

- Rosemary leaves mixed with an equal amount of honey is recommended for overcoming vomiting tendency.

- A cup of hot water taken before meals helps to prevent nausea to quite an extent.

MYTHS

Depression is always a response to a bad life situation.

FACTS

Not always, sometimes it may be associated with a chemical imbalance in your brain.

NOSE BLEEDING

- If it is a chronic problem, a daily intake of *gulkand* is extremely beneficial.

- Make a *murabba* out of *amla* and eat a piece every morning.

- For immediate relief, apply a bandage dipped in ice water on nose and the forehead.

MYTHS

Cataract worsens by reading, sewing or watching too much T.V.

FACTS

Reading or sewing does not affect the eyes. It is poor lighting or bad posture or not allowing the eyes to rest in between that aggravate cataract.

OBESITY

- Taking lime juice and honey water on empty stomach is highly beneficial in the treatment of obesity.

- Cabbage is considered an excellent home remedy for checking obesity.

- Tomatoes are valuable in controlling obesity. One or two ripe tomatoes taken early morning as a substitute for breakfast, for a couple of months, will help in inducing considerable weight reduction.

MYTHS

Air-filtering devices reduce pollution.

FACTS

These don't remove gaseous pollutants or very fine particulates from air, and are not known to provide any health benefits. They are promoted as 'air-purifiers', but in fact they may produce ozone, a dangerous pollutant.

OBESITY

Ardha-Matsyendrasana

This *asana* is useful in checking obesity.

1. Sit on the ground and spread the left leg in front of you.
2. Place the right foot on the side of your left knee.
3. Breathe in.
4. Pass your left arm around the right knee and hold your foot with your left hand. Take your right hand behind your back.
5. Turn the head and the trunk to your right as far as it can go, while exhaling, tilt the turned head downwards ensuring that the knee of the left leg does not rise from the ground.
6. Hold for six seconds in a period of suspension.
7. Release your hands and unwind the trunk, breathing in.
8. Repeat the same with the right leg stretched and putting the left foot beside the right knee.

PEPTIC ULCER

- Banana is one of the most effective home remedies for treating peptic ulcer.

- Lime is effective in curing peptic ulcers. The citric acid in the fruit, together with the mineral salts present in the juice, helps digestion.

- Tea prepared from fenugreek seeds is yet another useful remedy for controlling peptic ulcer.

MYTHS

Carbohydrates can make you fat.

FACTS

The idea that carbohydrates can lead to deposition of fats in your body is simply not true. But if a person is insulin-resistant then he/she might gain weight as a result of eating carbohydrates.

51

REMEDY FOR

PILES

- Consumption of dry figs is one of the most effective remedies for piles. Three or four figs should be soaked overnight in water after being cleaned thoroughly in hot water. Then first thing in the morning, drink the juice and eat the pulp.

- Mango seeds are an effective remedy for bleeding piles. The seeds should be collected during the mango season, dried in the shade, powered, and kept stored for use as medicine, whenever the need arises.

- *Sarvangasana (see page 38) is useful in curing piles.*

MYTHS

Honey is good for infants.

FACTS

Children under 12 months old should not be given honey as it may cause a form of food poisoning called botulism.

REMEDY FOR

PNEUMONIA

- During the early acute stage of pneumonia, tea made with fenugreek seeds induces the body to produce perspiration, which shortens the duration of fever.

- Garlic, is a marvellous remedy for pneumonia, if given in sufficient quantities. It brings down the temperature, as well as the pulse and respiration rates. A paste of garlic applied externally on the chest proves beneficial as it is an irritant and a rubefacient.

MYTHS

Dairy products like milk should be avoided since they make you fat.

FACTS

Actually, everyone needs dairy products in their diet, since they are a major source of calcium, which promotes bone growth.

REMEDY FOR

POOR MEMORY

- Rosemary helps to improve the blood supply to the head and thus improves one's memory besides stimulating the brain.

- Another remedy is to drink a tea made from sage, sweetened to taste, to improve memory.

- Hawthorn also improves the fading memory caused due to the ageing process or poor blood supply to the brain.

MYTHS

Tea is bad for your health.

FACTS

Research proves tea has manganese that increases the activity of the killer immune cells.

REMEDY FOR

PREMATURE GREYING HAIR

- Use of Indian gooseberry is a leading home remedy for prevention of greying of hair. The fruit, cut into pieces, should be dried and boiled in coconut oil till the solid matter becomes charred dust. Application of this dark coloured oil is very useful in preventing premature greying.

- Amaranth is another effective remedy for hair disorders. Application of fresh juice of *amarnath* leaves helps the hair to retain its normal black colour.

- Liberal intake of curry leaves also helps premature greying of hair.

MYTHS

Intake of low fat food won't make you fat.

FACTS

This is not exactly true because there are some food stuff which are low in fat but high in calories. Extra calories mean deposition of fats in the body.

RINGWORM

- An ideal cure for ringworm is to apply carbonate of soda and strong vinegar on the affected area.
- Another remedy involves cutting the hair from the affected area and rubbing in turpentine. Finally the affected area is washed off with carbolic soap.

MYTHS

All fast foods are junk food.

FACTS

Not necessarily, if chosen properly even a pizza with cheese, mushrooms, onions or any other fast food may be quiet nutritious.

SORE THROAT

- Bishop's weed or *ajwain* is valuable in treating a sore throat. An infusion of the seeds mixed with common salt can be used beneficially as a gargle in an acute condition.

- Cinnamon is also effective in checking sore throat. One teaspoon of coarsely powdered cinnamon, boiled in a glass of water with a pinch of pepper powder and two teaspoons of honey, can be taken as medicine for treatment of this condition.

MYTHS

Vegetarians don't get enough protein.

FACTS

Vegetarians get proteins from sources like grains and soya beans unlike non-vegetarians who get them from meats and eggs.

REMEDY FOR

STRESS

- Basil leaves have been found beneficial in the treatment of stress. The patient should take four leaves twice daily, for preventing stress.

- Vitamin A found in green and yellow vegetables, and Vitamin B found in nuts, green leafy vegetables, yeast, sprouts and bananas should be taken to prevent stress.

- Yoghurt, blackstrap molasses, seeds and sprouts are quite beneficial in lessening stress.

MYTHS

Fasting for long periods can lead to weight loss.

FACTS

If you fast for a long period you will lose only muscle mass and not fats. Also the body requires some amount of nutrients to continue its daily operations.

STRESS

Tadasana

This *asana* is useful for overcoming stress.

1. Bring the feet together. Heels, big toes and knees should touch each other.
2. Keep the hands straight beside the body.
3. The back, shoulder, neck, chest and abdomen should be kept straight and erect.
4. Look straight. Breathe normally.
5. Remain in the same posture for 30 seconds.
6. Repeat three to five times.

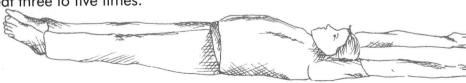

REMEDY FOR

STIFFNESS

- A remedy for stiffness occurring after strenuous exercise involves soaking in a bath of hot water as hot as can be comfortably tolerated for at least ten minutes. Then a little camphorated oil is rubbed on the skin and kneaded into the muscles.

- Salicylate of soda can be taken before going to bed for loosening the limbs and for stiffness.

MYTHS

Excess weight is as bad as ill health and exercise which does not lead to weight loss for obese people is of no use.

FACTS

Diabetes, high cholesterol etc mean ill health. Exercise, even if it does not reduce weight immediately, helps the body fight all abnormalities.

STINGS

- Crushed garlic or garlic macerated in oil can be rubbed on the sting.

- Cinnamon, oil of cardamom can also be used for obtaining relief in case of stings.

- In case of stings by bees, was ps, hornets, it is advisable to first extract the sting and then rub olive oil on the affected area.

- Honey applied on an area stung by bee can help to offset the effect of the sting.

MYTHS

People with asthma should not exercise.

FACTS

Rather exercise, when approached in a relaxed manner increases physical tolerance by boosting the level of gamma interferon.

STOMACH PAIN

- Application of heat on the stomach is an effective remedy for curing stomach ache.
- Peppermint is also instrumental in curing abdominal pains and spasms.
- Another remedy involves heating a pint of milk and then adding four teaspoons of brandy before being given to the patient.

MYTHS

Raw vegetables provide more iron to your body than cooked vegetables.

FACTS

Rather, cooking vegetables makes it easier for your body to absorb the iron they contain, however, cooked vegetables should be eaten at the earliest possible.

SUNSTROKE

- The best remedy for sunstroke is to drink a little juice of raw mango along with salt and sugar. Have this twice or thrice a day.

- You could also apply onion slices on your head and forehead as this has a cooling effect. Drink lots of fluids.

- To prevent sunstroke, a cabbage leaf kept inside the crown of a hat, can prove very beneficial.

MYTHS

White table sugar is worse than most natural sweeteners like brown sugar, fruit sugar, honey or jaggery.

FACTS

All of these essentially supply nothing but nutritionally empty calories.

TONSILLITIS

- A fresh lime squeezed in a glass of warm water, with four teaspoons of honey and a quarter teaspoon of common salt, should be taken to prevent tonsillitis.

- A glass of pure boiled milk, mixed with a pinch of turmeric powder and pepper powder, should be drunk daily for three nights to cure tonsillitis.

- Juices of carrot, beet and cucumber, taken individually or in combination, are especially beneficial.

- *Sarvangasana (see page 38) is useful in curing tonsillitis*

Sarvangasana (see page 38)

MYTHS

If I take food supplements then I don't need to eat much.

FACTS

Don't ever use food supplements as a replacement for a meal.

REMEDY FOR

TOOTHACHE

- Chew a piece of clove or dip a piece of cotton wool in clove oil and place it on the aching tooth for quick relief.

- Fresh ginger can be chewed to dull the pain of toothache. Ground ginger can be mixed with Epsom salts and added to hot water to try an alternative remedy.

- Dip a piece of cotton wool in onion juice and apply it to the aching tooth.

MYTHS

Cholesterol is bad for health.

FACTS

While bad cholesterol blocks your arteries, good cholesterol fights and removes bad cholesterol. Saturated fats kill good cholesterol so they should be avoided.

UNDERWEIGHT

- Mango-milk proves an ideal treatment for being underweight. In this mode of treatment, sweet mangoes should be taken and then followed with a glass of milk.

- Figs are also an excellent measure for increasing weight. The high percentage of the rapidly assimilable sugar in this fruit makes it a strengthening and fattening food.

- More of sweets and sugar tend to increase ones's weight, provided too much exercise is not done for that burns away the calories.

MYTHS

Vegetarianism is all right for adults, but kids need meat to grow properly.

FACTS

No, they don't. And children don't necessarily need eggs either.